Rockstar Headlife
by
Nikeema T. Lee

FORWARD

It's all about creating. You are now creating the space for your desires. You have been divinely guided to this book. You now see clear to your path of success. Thank you Thank you Thank you

Fear is an Illusion

Be Yourself

Be Self-Assured

Be Wise

Be Faithful

Be In Courage

Be Allowing

Be Authentic

TABLE OF CONTENTS

ROCKSTAR SEXLIFE

The following is an excerpt from the book Rockstar Sexlife. The content can be read in its entirety by purchasing Rockstar Sexlife from www.nikeemalee.com

CHAPTER 6

"Clinton lied. A man might forget where he parks or where he lives, but he never forgets oral sex, no matter how bad it is."

Barbara Bush - Former First Lady of the United States of America

ELEVATION OF SKILLS

WOW!! What a ride. You have explored so much about yourself. Mastering, Accepting and Demanding. You are 95% of the way to having a Rockstar Sexlife. Yes sex is 95% mental, spiritual and emotional and only 5% physical. Now that we have address the issues that block you from trusting and accepting, we can get to the deliciousness of sex. The sweaty, raw and intoxicating part of sex. Elevating your skills is the final step to having a Rockstar sexlife. I love this part of the book and will start me my favorite topic.

FELLATIO!

How many dick suckers are reading this? Haha... If hearing that word makes you blush or offended then you shouldn't be having sex at all. This book is meant to help you lose the last bit of obstacles that can be holding you back from opening up completely. Knowing more about your partner is nothing compared to learning more about yourself. Now back to our lesson in oral stimulation.

The Blowjob

There isn't a man alive who wouldn't sell his soul for an amazing blowjob. You may feel that you already have a killer head game, and I have no doubt you do, however you may read on a find a few tips that will help catapult your Mic skills to new heights. If you're a beginner, read the tips and choose two or three suggestions you would like to try. Remember not ever tip, tool and technique is for you and will bring pleasure to your partner, so try them all and PRACTICE, PRACTICE, PRACTICE.

Rule # 11
Practice, Practice, Practice

Also take into account that as we get older and have different sexual partners, our needs will change and evolve so if you have been in a relationship for a significant amount of time trying something new for your partner may open uncharted doors that can lead to great sexual satisfaction. I know that many of you participate in then act and wonder how you can improve on your performance. Well this book is here to show you a few tips that you need to have in order to take your blowjob skills to Rockstar status.

MASTER YOUR PARTNER

Mastering your partner is simply...learning them.

THE ANATOMY

Do you know all the parts of the penis? I bet you don't. Test your knowledge by matching the parts of the penis to their description.

Glans	The area between the anus and the testicles
Frenulum	Where sperm is made and stored for ejaculation
Shaft	The most sensitive part of the penis
Perineum	The Head of the penis
Testicles	The length of the penis

Check the Chapter Summary for the answers. How did you do? Do you know your penis?

Rate of score

0-1: you are penis **NOVICE** and I believe you may even be a virgin. It's completely OK. However this book may make you into a complete expect by the time you are finish

2-4: you are a **PRO** and you know your penis. Keep reading for a great way to use your knowledge

5: You are an **EXPECT** on all things male reproduction and your knowledge of your partner is going to make you a bona fide Rockstar in no time, so keep reading.

So now that you know the anatomy of your partner, get to know then personally. Please note that every man is different and will experience different things with different woman for different reasons. Don't get so wrapped up in a technique that you can't give your partner pleasure because you have the moves of Peter and Tom mastered but you're now with Phil and he desires something totally different. When you take the time to learn what your current partner needs, wants and or desires you are 95% of the way to Rockstar status with your current mate.

Blowjobs aren't just for men's pleasure. Many women say the feeling of control and power combined with the pleasure she can give is a complete turn on. So in order to find pleasure for both you and your partner ask him if receiving a blowjob is something he desires. Some men hold different beliefs on the act and you may have stumbled upon one that has no desire to have is flesh slurped up by your vacuum jaws. So instead of wasting your mouth mileage on someone who would otherwise not receive this oral pleasure, ask them what they want.

By asking your partner you learn two things:
Whether you can or can't meet his demands.

You will have a clear picture of what the mandate on your time will be in order to pleasure your partner. A mature and honest man should be able to communicate his needs and desires to you.

ACCEPT THE CHALLENGE

Now that you have asked and he has answered, you can now ACCEPT or DECLINE the job. Get it… Blowjob! It's not just a casual thing. Remember that you are putting someone penis into your mouth. Now the penis is not the cleanest thing in the world. Men are dirty and the penis is no exception. Even the cleanest man can have sweaty, uncircumcised and even down right smelly penis any time of the day. Well maybe not uncircumcised but you get my point, you never know what you going to get. So knowing and accepting your level of commitment is essential. When you agree to accept your partner's needs you are accepting all of them. Making a full effort to provide your partner with a full array of the things they need is important to having a healthy relationship. You are either all in or all out.

That's why rule number 12 is important. The best head

Rule # 12
Never suck a dick you don't like

involves a giver who is totally into it, someone who is even aroused by doing it. So if you don't like, trust or believe in your partner, why suck their penis? Are you doing it for some other low level reason? Are you doing it so he will like you? Are you doing it so that you can keep him around?

CHAPTER SUMMARY

- This book is meant to help you lose the last bit of obstacles that can be holding you back from opening up completely.
- PRACTICE, PRACTICE, PRACTICE.
- Mastering your partner is simply...learning them.
- Do you know your penis?
  - Glans -The Head of the penis
  - Frenulum- The most sensitive part of the penis
  - Shaft-The length of the penis
  - Perineum-The area between the anus and the testicles
  - Testicles-Where sperm is made and stored for ejaculation
- Please note that every man is different and will experience different things with different woman for different reasons.
- When you take the time to learn what your current partner needs, wants and or desires you are 95% of the way to Rockstar status with your current mate.
- Blowjobs aren't just for men's pleasure. Women enjoy the power of pleasing their mate.
- By asking your partner you learn two things:
  - Whether you can or can't meet his demands.

CHAPTER SUMMARY

- A mature and honest man should be able to communicate his needs and desires to you.
- Penis sucking not just a casual thing. We are talking about putting human flesh into your mouth. Knowing and accepting your level of commitment is essential.
- When you agree to accept your partner's needs you are accepting all of them. Making a full effort to provide your partner with a full array of the things they need is important to having a healthy relationship. You are either all in or all out.
- If you don't like, trust or believe in your partner, why suck their penis?
- Are you doing it for some other low level reason? Are you doing it so he will like you? Are you doing it so that you can keep him around?

CHAPTER 7

"If sex were shoes, I'd wear you out. But I wouldn't wear you out in public."

— Jarod Kintz, American Author

DEMAND SATISFACTION

Now I'm talking to my people who have a worship of the penis and it's justified. You must find it extremely erotic to pleasure your partner in this way. You must enjoy the feeling of penis in your mouth, how it looks in your hands and how it stimulates you tongue. Getting off on the feeling of power you have over your lover as you control his pleasure, should give you a sexual charge and ultimately make you orgasm when you perform it. Whatever your drive, you must absolutely, positively be into giving this man the best blowjob of his life each and every time you perform, otherwise no one will enjoy it. It will be a complete waste of your mouth mileage and his penis time. Use your time wisely.

When it comes to giving head there are guidelines to performing it at the Rockstar level. You can take your skills to one man or many men and quickly determine what will work best for him.

Rule # 13
Giving Head saves lives

GIVE HEAD

Studies have proven that women who perform fellatio at least 2-3 times a week live a longer life. Now experts can determine whether it's the act itself or the heartfelt enjoyment that leads to a longer life. I believe in the latter. I believe that it's the joy that women get from pleasing her man in such a way that it gives her satisfaction. Performing the act of fellatio regularly is not only beneficially for the woman but it also helps to enhance the relationship bring couples together on a deeper intimate level more often.

EXPLORE HIS WHOLE BODY

Starting slow by touching, licking and kissing him will alert his brain that something is about to go down. Don't be afraid to explore is other pleasure zones like his nipples before heading to the targeted area. Being vocal also never hurt. Talking dirty to him is a great way to help focus your mind on the task at hand and gets him aroused quickly. The idea is to let him know you are really into doing this deed for him and to him.

USE YOUR WHOLE BODY

The best blowjob involve more than just your mouth, and focus on much more than just his penis. Use everything he has to please him. Again by using your whole body you show him that you are just as into the giving as he is into the receiving. Use not just your mouth but also your tongue, face, hair, hands, nails and even chest to heighten his experience. Rubbing is penis against your vagina can be the ultimate stimulator but be careful not to get to carried away that you stick it in and forget to actually perform fellatio. Try not to over think your movements and let your body and mind get in sync with the rhythm of his body naturally.

START SLOW

When you first encounter his penis, remember to move slowly. Take your time and get acquainted with it. If it's flaccid, and it shouldn't be if you have employed the skills from above, however if you have skipped those steps go back and use them, they are important to giving a Rockstar blowjob. With your hands, mouth and tongue, explore every inch of his stiffness. Run your tongue along his shaft, remembering to give a little eye contact in the process. This will help to maintain the intimate connection you are looking to build by doing this in the first place.

BE CREATIVE

There is no exact play by play that you must to do, so allow yourself to be swept away in the magic energy of your work. You are the painter and his penis is your canvas. Lick and suck your way to a masterpiece. Run your tongue along his shaft, noting the texture of each vein and bulge. Run your tongue along is testicles, placing them in your mouth and sucking them. Monitor his responses so you know what he likes without him even having to tell you. Try to move seamlessly from his shaft to the head of his penis. Make your movement effortless. Every man is different; the same man might love a gentle touch one night and may want you to bite his penis another…literally "bite my penis." Don't be afraid to try something new. If he likes it, his body will let you know. If he doesn't, just pay attention and move on to something else.

CHAPTER SUMMARY

- You must enjoy the feeling of penis in your mouth, how it looks in your hands and how it stimulates you tongue. Getting off on the feeling of power you have over your lover as you control his pleasure, should give you a sexual charge and ultimately make you orgasm when you perform it.

- Whatever your drive, you must absolutely, positively be into giving this man the best blowjob of his life each and every time you perform, otherwise no one will enjoy it.

- GIVE HEAD Studies have proven that women who perform fellatio at least 2-3 times a week live a longer life.

- Rule # Giving Head saves lives

- Explore His Whole Body. Starting slow by touching, licking and kissing him will alert his brain that something is about to go down.

- Use your Whole Body. The best blowjob involve more than just your mouth, and focus on much more than just his penis.

CHAPTER SUMMARY

- Start Slow. When you first encounter his penis, remember to move slowly. Take your time and get acquainted with it.
- Be Creative. There is no exact play by play that you must to do, so allow yourself to be swept away in the magic energy of your work. You are the painter and his penis is your canvas.

CHAPTER 8

"The main reason Santa is so jolly is because he knows where all the bad girls live."

— *George Carlin, American Comedian*

DEEP THROAT

We will get back to more tips for penis pleasure. The topic of deep throating is so intense it had to get it's own chapter. Be slick at this point and add your personal lubrication to his penis. Don't waste your time finding silicone based lubes or something flavored. You can produce all that you need in order to grasp the ultimate Rockstar experience. The process of deep throating his penis is a complete turn on for him. Seeing you take a large part if not all of his penis into your mouth will send electric charges through his body and make you the ruler of his penis.

THE THROAT

If you want to relax your throat, guess what, drinking alcohol will not help. Alcohol actually tightens the throat muscles. This is especially true for spirits, so steer clear if you want to have an enjoyable experience. Many have long believe that getting drunk will help you have a better time while having sex, when in fact it takes away from the wonderful feeling. Besides, if you're a bit on the tipsy side you may not be aware of whether or not if he is actually enjoying your performance!

Another great technique is to breath. As penis goes further down your throat your ability to exchange carbon dioxide for oxygen is limited. If you want to breathe do it through your nose.

Finally, get that throat wide open. The best technique to do this is to exhale. Remember to exhale *before* you take his penis in your mouth. This will increase your oral capacity by about 33%. Try it. Take a deep breath in. Notice that the tongue draws itself up and in. Now exhale, see how the mouth opens up and relaxes.

Now let's tackle the ugly elephant in the room, the dreaded gag reflex. When deep throating the penis you will inevitable encounter the dreaded gag reflex. The pharyngeal reflex or gag reflex (also known as a laryngeal spasm) is a reflex contraction of the back of the throat. It's evoked by touching the roof of the mouth, the back of the tongue, the area around the tonsils and the back of the throat. The gag reflex prevents something from entering the throat except as part of normal swallowing and helps prevent choking.

Because our bodies are built for survival the brain will sense the trigger of your gag reflex as a call for help and in doing so will produce saliva in order to help free the throat from the obstruction. This nature pool of lube can be used to help you take his penis further down your throat.

As a deep throat expert I have listed the

TOP 10 WAYS YOU CAN REDUCE YOUR GAG REFLEX FOR A BETTER FELLATIO EXPERIENCE:

1. Numb your soft palate. When an object touches the soft palate (far back in the roof of your mouth), it can trigger the gag reflex, so you can use a numbing throat spray to desensitize the soft palate, or a gel that's normally used to relieve tooth pain. The effects should last for about an hour, and your soft palate will be less reactive.

2. Disengage your gag reflex. By gradually getting your soft palate accustomed to being touched, you can minimize the gag reflex, or perhaps even get rid of it completely. This is the first step that sword swallower must take and it does require effort and patience over time.

3. Relax. The gag reflex is triggered by a combination of psychology and physiology. For some people, the psychological aspect will play a larger role. Maybe you've had a traumatizing experience at a doctor or dentist's office in the past, or in general, you have a fear of losing control. Some steps such as controlled breathing, will help. You may also want to practice some form of meditation. In more extreme situations, some people find hypnosis works.

4. Lift both of your legs if you're sitting or lying down on your back. Tightening your abdominal muscles might help stop gagging.

5. Make a fist. Close your left thumb in your left hand and make a fist. Squeeze tight.

6. Put a little table salt on your tongue. Moisten the tip of your finger, dip it into some salt, and dab the tip of your tongue with that. Another way to do this is to put a teaspoon of salt in a glass of water, and rinse your mouth with that. Don't forget to spit!

7. Hum. You might find that it's difficult to gag and hum at the same time.

8. Listen to music. Distracting your mind can help keep it from giving too much focus to that which gags you.

9. Beware the gag reflex in the morning. Some people report that they're more likely to gag earlier in the day. Try to schedule the gag-inducing activity for the late afternoon or evening instead.

10. Breathe through your nose. Taking a nasal decongestant beforehand can help clear the nasal passageways and facilitate breathing, if your nose is congested. This method may not be a good idea if it's a foul smell that's triggering your gag reflex.

WARNING:

REMEMBER THAT THE GAG REFLEX IS YOUR BODY'S WAY OF PROTECTING YOU FROM CHOKING.

When disengaging the gag reflex with a toothbrush, don't start too far back. It is possible to desensitize a farther point in your tongue without first treating a spot toward the front and this isn't what you're trying to achieve.

CONSULT YOUR DOCTOR.

Excessive gagging could be a sign of a more serious condition, like GERD (Gastro Esophageal Reflux Disease), which has to do with your stomach and the acid levels in it.

CHAPTER SUMMARY

- The topic of Deep throating is so intense it had to get it's own chapter.

- The process of deep throating his penis is the complete turn on for him.

- When deep throating the penis you will inevitable encounter the dreaded gag reflex.

- The pharyngeal reflex or gag reflex (also known as a laryngeal spasm) is a reflex contraction of the back of the throat.

- Because our bodies are built for survival the brain will sense the trigger of your gag reflex as a call for help and in doing so will produce saliva in order to help free the throat from the obstruction.

- The top 10 ways you can reduce your gag reflex for a better fellatio experience:
  - **1. Numb your soft palate.**
  - **2. Disengage your gag reflex.**
  - **3. Relax**.
  - **4. Lift both of your legs if you're sitting or lying down on your back**.
  - **5. Make a fist.**

CHAPTER SUMMARY

- **6. Put a little table salt on your tongue.**
- **7. Hum.**
- **8. Listen to music.**
- **9. Beware the gag reflex in the morning.**
- **10. Breathe through your nose.**

- Warning: Remember that the gag reflex is your body's way of protecting you from choking.

- Consult your doctor. Excessive gagging could be a sign of a more serious condition, like GERD (Gastro esophageal Reflux Disease), which has to do with your stomach and the acid levels in it.

CHAPTER 9

"Flirting is a woman's trade, one must keep in practice."

— *Charlotte Brontë, Jane Eyre*

BEYOND SUCKING

Licking and nibbling is quite stimulating, so do it. Running your tongue around the glans, and then focus on the frenulum, this is his most sensitive part. Flick your tongue back and forth and all around the head of his penis while you are sucking, this will blow his mind. Don't forget to lick the bottom of his shaft while you slowing rub the head of his penis. Now with all this effort on your part is your partner quiet and even still? No worries. Pay no attention to his verbal cues but more to his no verbal gestures. Take a look at his testicles. When they are aroused they will rise up into his scrotum. So rather than hanging they will draw up like two scared cats pressed up against his thighs.

BE RESOURCEFUL

Try not to be miss bobble head. Do not simply move your head up and down on the shaft. Yeah you will get results but we are talking about giving a Rockstar blowjob, your skills must be advanced. Understand that your mouth and hands are more capable of providing different levels of pleasure than your vagina and anus.

Stick your tongue out and say "ah." Leave your tongue out of your mouth and use it to pleasure his tip as you stroke. As I mentioned before when you stick your tongue out to exhale you open your mouth wider. Although the shaft has less nerves that his tip, they sure do enjoy the sensation. Using your tongue and even lips will help to simulate him so intensely. Moaning when you do this will create a vibrating effect on his penis. Long before Hummer was a popular car, women were pleasing their partners by using this technique to send shooting stimuli though the bodies of men.

TRY SOME MOVES

Draw your lips into a tight circle, so there is almost a popping sound when the head moves in and out. WATCH YOUR TEETH! Once the action builds can easily cause injury if your not careful. However, some men like the feel if teeth and some even like for you to bite their penis. YES! "bite me bitch." Don't stop to look at him crazy that just what he likes and your there to please.

Try sucking his penis and creating a vacuum-like tightness and pressure. Don't be afraid to suck hard, as many men enjoy that strong sensation. Such on the head, or take the whole dick in your mouth and maintain the suction the entire time you slide it in and out of your month. Be open-minded and playful. As you practice you will find more way to please your partner.

GOOD VIBRATIONS

Add a little vibration to the your sucking. Yes you can hum on the penis but your mouth will never be as powerful as a battery. If you hold and bullet to your jaw while you suck you r entire head will vibrate. Vibrating cock rings are also a great way to provide this intense feeling.

Warning: Please don't keep a cockring on the penis for NO MORE than 20 minutes. The penis is exposed to extended periods of constriction can cause damage.

KNOCK AT HIS BACK DOOR

Many men enjoy anal stimulation. While your mouth is busy with his penis, gently touch his anus with the tip of your finger. If you get no kickback, insert that finger deep into his anus. If he response positively work that finger and your mouth and the same time. When your inside his anus you don't want to be to rough unless he wants you to. Search for his Prostate and add pressure. The Prostate feels just like the G-Spot on a woman and doesn't require much to stimulate it. Just press your finger upon it. He will respond to your advances, let him lead you. Use your other hand to press against the perineum, the area between the base of the penis and his anus. With these two areas stimulated you can bring great pleasure to his Prostate.

Many men are driven completely mad by this approach. If he enjoys rectal stimulation, you can take his dick into your mouth while facing him, then wrap your arms around his hips and use both hands to stimulate his rectum and anus. Hugging him towards you every time you take his penis deep into your mouth. Talk about multi-tasking.

THE CRESCENDO

By now probably you both have worked up a head of serious sexual steam and if your following the steps listed above you are a Rockstar Cockstar. If you feel he is approaching climax (i.e., his toes are curled, clutching the sheets, the neighbors know your name and he's proposed marriage a few time--a sure sign that you are doing things right), then you might want to slow down and let penis/vaginal action take place.

THE MOMENT OF TRUTH

Assume the position. Any position. When you sense he is ready to cum, quicken the pace. You should be pumping fast and furiously with your mouth and hands. DO NOT SLOW DOWN. You have to be totally committed at this point. Give him everything all at once. Head play, balls, anal, whatever it takes to get him to explode his load.

As he nears orgasm, you will notice changes. His breathing, quick and shallow; his muscles, tense and contracted; his balls, draw close to the body; his shaft, rock hard...KEEP PUMPING.

TO SWALLOW OR NOT TO SWALLOW

To Spit or to Swallow

- It's your decision: some like to take cum into their mouth, some like to watch it shoot. Both can be sexy.
- If you choose to take it in your mouth, you can swallow or keep a cloth or napkin nearby to spit into.
- Know your partner and make good choices. Swallowing during oral sex on a HOV-infected man can been know to transmit the virus

Most men enjoy it when you swallow their cum. Men who have strong feelings for their lovers in particular may report feelings of intimacy and acceptance when you swallow. Many find it difficult to swallow. Remember that its only a small amount of liquid, about a teaspoon or so. The taste of semen varies form person to person. If you don't like the taste change your partner diet.

If you find it difficult to swallow you may try holding your breath and swallowing quickly. Like taking a pill or medicine.

Some people find it easier to deep throat at the point of ejaculation, this bypasses the taste buds.

If you find that none of these methods work for you, its ok. Just hold the cum in your mouth and spit it out or let him cum on your face or body. Either way he will be pleased with your experience and you will be a total Rockstar.

CHAPTER SUMMARY

- Licking and nibbling is quite stimulating, so do it. Running your tongue around the glans, and then focus on the frenulum, this is his most sensitive part.
- Try not to be miss bobble head. Do not simply move your head up and down on the shaft.
- Stick your tongue out and say "ah." Leave your tongue out of your mouth and use it to pleasure his tip as you stroke.
- Draw your lips into a tight circle, so there is almost a popping sound when the head moves in and out.
- WATCH YOUR TEETH!
- Try sucking his penis and creating a vacuum-like tightness and pressure. Don't be afraid to suck hard, as many men enjoy that strong sensation.
- Add a little vibration to the your sucking.
- **Warning: Please don't keep a cockring on the penis for NO MORE than 20 minutes. The penis is exposed to extended periods of constriction can cause damage.**

CHAPTER SUMMARY

- Many men enjoy anal stimulation. While your mouth is busy with his penis, gently touch his anus with the tip of your finger.

- The Prostate feels just like the G-Spot on a woman and doesn't require much to stimulate it.

- If you feel he is approaching climax (i.e., his toes are curled, clutching the sheets, the neighbors know your name and he's proposed marriage a few time--a sure sign that you are doing things right), then you might want to slow down and let penis/vaginal action take place.

- When you sense he is ready to cum, quicken the pace.

- As he nears orgasm, you will notice changes. His breathing, quick and shallow; his muscles, tense and contracted; his balls, draw close to the body; his shaft, rock hard...KEEP PUMPING.

- To Spit or to Swallow
  - It's your decision: some like to take cum into their mouth, some like to watch it shoot. Both can be sexy.

CHAPTER SUMMARY

- If you choose to take it in your mouth, you can swallow or keep a cloth or napkin nearby to spit into.
- Know your partner and make good choices. Swallowing during oral sex on a HOV-infected man can been know to transmit the virus
- Most men enjoy it when you swallow their cum.
- The taste of semen varies form person to person.
- If you find it difficult to swallow you may try holding your breath and swallowing quickly. Like taking a pill or medicine. Some people find it easier to deep throat at the point of ejaculation, this bypasses the taste buds.
- If you find that none of these methods work for you, its ok. Just hold the cum in your mouth and spit it out or let him cum on your face or body. Either way he will be pleased with your experience and you will be a total Rockstar.

ROCKSTAR HEADLIFE
HANDBOOK

Is there a man alive who wouldn't sell his soul for a killer blowjob? Even if you feel you give damn good fellatio already, you may find something in this workshop that may further blow your man's mind. If you are a novice, read the tips and choose two or three suggestions you would like to try. Not everything here will appeal to you or your lover. But everyone's sexuality changes and evolves with time, so there is room for growth and learning in your encounters even with a longtime partner.

Blowjobs aren't just for men's pleasure. Many women say the feeling of control it gives them combined with the oral stimulation is a turn-on in its own right. And the more it turns her on, the more exciting it is for him. Read on for tips and techniques to make a blowjob an ultimately satisfying experience for all involved.

The Anatomy

- Know what you're getting into:
- Glans: The head of the penis
- Frenulum: The underside of the glans; ** the most sensitive part **
- Shaft: The length of the penis
- Perineum: The area between the anus and the testicles
- Testicles: Where sperm is made and stored for ejaculation.

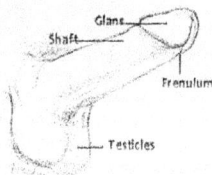

Condoms

While oral sex can be a fulfilling form of contraception, it is not without risk of disease. Unless you are monogamous and have both recently tested negative for HIV and other STDs, plan to use a condom. Be sure to put it on his penis after he is hard and before you have oral, anal, or genital contact with his penis. Choose from an almost endless variety of condoms – colored, ribbed, flavored, whatever you like. Put a small amount of a *petroleum-free lube* (it won't degrade the condom) on the inside tip of the condom before putting it on your partner. Learn to put one on with just your teeth, tongue, lips, and mouth (you can practice on a dildo.) Put the condom on in this manner as he watches, making plenty of eye contact with him as you do so. Drizzle lots of lube on the outside of the condom and rub it on with your hands

Show enthusiasm.

The best fellatio involves a giver who is totally into it, aroused, even a little worshipful. You may find it extremely erotic to pleasure your partner in this way. You may enjoy the stimulation to your lips, tongue, mouth, and hands as you perform a blowjob. Perhaps you get off on the feeling of power you have over your lover as you control his pleasure, or you may get a sexual charge out of feeling dominated by your lover as you serve him. Maybe you enjoy the sense of giving involved in this extremely intimate act. Whatever your scene, you absolutely, positively must be into giving this man a blowjob, otherwise no one will enjoy it.

Set the scene.

Although a quickie blowjob in an elevator certainly should have its place in your sexual repertoire, most men will enjoy a blowjob to the fullest in a more relaxed setting. The best oral sex begins long before you take off his clothes. Wear something you know he finds sexy on you. Help him to relax and loosen up, perhaps with a bath or a glass of wine together. Keep the lighting soft, light a few candles. Choose music that is not distracting, but rather blends quietly into the background. Turn the TV off ... unless you want to add porn to the mix. If you do, you may find "compilation videos" or hard-core segments less distracting than porn laden with plot and dialogue.

Lay him on his back on a large bed with clean, crisp sheets. Slowly undress him. By taking your time, you build his anticipation and arousal to a tantalizing level. Make sure he has no distractions whatsoever. Turn off the phones, lock the door. Make sure everything you need is within easy reach: condoms, lube, sex toys, something to drink, and something refreshing to eat (perhaps a bowl of fresh strawberries, chilled grapes, or orange slices). Let him focus entirely on his pleasure. If he touches you, it should be for his own enjoyment and not to pleasure you. Make it clear that he is in for a real treat.

Explore his whole body.

Start slowly. Touch, lick, and kiss your partner, not just the areas that turn him on but the ones that turn you on as well: the nape of his neck, his earlobes, his chest, his nipples, his round buttocks, feet and sensitive toes, thighs. Be vocal about the areas you adore, either by moaning with pleasure or simply telling him how hot you find his hard biceps, for instance. Talk dirty to him if you enjoy doing so. The idea is to let him know how much you relish contact with him. Keep exploring as you gradually work your way to his genitals. Try licking and sucking his fingers so he gets a preview of what is in store for his cock. Take your time and savor his entire body.

Use your whole body.

The best blowjobs involve much more than just your mouth, and focus on much more than just his penis. Use everything available to you to pleasure him. (Also, by using your whole body you show your own arousal and enthusiasm.) Use your mouth, lips, tongue, face, hair, hands, fingers and nails, chest, whatever occurs to you. Rub your genitals against his cock, his leg, or his hand in order to increase your own arousal during the blowjob. Let your body move naturally along with the movement of your mouth and hands. Allow it to be a sensual dance. He's likely to enjoy the show.

Basic Up & Down

* Position yourself comfortably;
* Start by teasing his penis - kiss, breathe lightly, whisper, tickle.
* Switch to sucking. Create a vacuum by pursing your lips, then using them to surround his penis.
* Thrust your mouth down over his penis while you suck.
* Use your saliva as a lubricant.
* Stroke with your hands while sucking.
* Twist your hand as you move up and down on the shaft.
* Switch hands occasionally for variation

Start slowly. When you first encounter his cock, move slowly. Get acquainted with it. If it's flaccid, place it in your mouth and explore it with your tongue. Delight in the sensation of it getting large and stiff within your mouth. With your hands, mouth and tongue, explore every inch of it. Run your tongue along the shaft, note the texture, each vein and bulge. Run your tongue along his testicles, explore the difference in texture there, place a testicle in your mouth and suck. Observe his response. Some men adore having their balls licked and sucked.

Move back up the shaft slowly, working your way to the head. Remember to make eye contact with your lover. You may both find it powerfully erotic to gaze into each other's eyes as you perform this intimate act. Use your tongue to explore the ridge where the head meets the shaft. Pay particular attention to the frenulum, which is the loose patch of skin on the underside of the penis where the head meets the shaft. Most men find this an intensely sensitive area. Run your tongue along it, first gently, then a little harder. Kiss it, suck at it. Gauge his response.

Move on to the head. Wet it with your mouth. Feel the smooth, hard surface against your lips, kiss it, lick it, tease it ever so gently with your teeth (if you are using a condom, be careful not to puncture it). Explore the hole in the center of the head with your tongue. This hole is called the meatus, and it's where urine and semen come out of the penis. Some men enjoy stimulation to this area. Now slowly take the hard, sensitive head entirely in your mouth while using your tongue to stimulate the frenulum. If your partner is seated or lying down, and you are between his legs facing him, your tongue can easily stimulate the frenulum on the underside of the penis as you move the head in and out of your mouth. Pull the head out of your mouth and flick your tongue rapidly against the frenulum. Some men really get off on this sensation.

Be Creative.

There is no script. So allow yourself to be swept away by the moment and do what feels good to you and your partner. Explore different ways of pleasuring your partner. Every man is different, and every encounter is different: the same man might love a gentle touch one night, but want more aggressive play another night. Don't be afraid to try new things. But always pay close attention to the response of your lover. If you try something new and he squirms and moans with pleasure, keep at it. If not, move on to something else.

Begin to build and increase the action. Play around with different moves and see to what he responds, what his mood is for that session. When you find something he enjoys, stay with it for a few minutes or longer, then vary it. If he really loved something you did, you can return to it later. But never do the exact same things for an extended period, as the effect of even the most wonderful sensations diminish with time.

Be slick. At this point, you may want to apply lube to his nice erect cock, even if you are not using a condom. This process in itself can be quite entertaining. Drip the lube slowly along his head and shaft, and then use your hands to cover his penis with it. Be sure to choose a lube that is tasteless and odorless or one who's taste and smell you like. We like the silicone lube **Pjur Eros Body Glide**. It is odorless, has no taste whatsoever, never gets sticky, and is highly concentrated so a little lasts a long time. Enjoy the feel of his slick rod in your hands and mouth.

Beyond Sucking

- Licking & nibbling is quite stimulating.
- Run your tongue around the glans, and then focus on the frenulum.
- Flick your tongue back and forth and all around as you're sucking.
- Lick the bottom of the shaft while using your hand to fondle the glans, and vice versa.

Do you have a lover who tends to be quiet and still? How can you tell if he likes what you're doing? Notice his testicles. When he is aroused, his testicles will rise within the scrotum, so rather than two balls hanging in a loose sac, the balls will be high against the base of the penis and the scrotum stretched tightly across them. Also, his cock will be very stiff and the head will swell even further and become rock hard. Pay attention to these signs that you are pleasing him.

Try different moods. Be playful, intense, slow and sensual, or fast and frantic—or all these things in turns during a great blowjob. Relax and follow your instincts, and take your cues from your partner.

Be resourceful.

Try not to have your head simply bobbing up and down on the shaft. This action may produce results, but we're talking about more advanced skills here. You aren't merely simulating intercourse. Your mouth and hands have a great many more ways to pleasure his cock than has a pussy or anus. So go ahead and stroke away, but vary it.

Stick out your tongue and say "ah." Leave your tongue out of your mouth and use it to pleasure his frenulum as you stroke. Also by sticking your tongue out, you can take the shaft deeper into your mouth.

All-Around Focus

- There's more to the penis than meets the eye:
- Take his balls gently into your mouth and suck.
- Run your tongue along his perineum.
- Lick his anus and see if he likes it.
- Rub his balls gently as you suck the shaft.

Although the shaft has far fewer nerve endings than the head and the frenulum, many men adore the sensation of being taken fully into their lover's mouth and even their throat. When you are stroking him with your mouth, don't forget to use your tongue and lips to increase the sensation. Try sticking your tongue out so you lick his shaft as you stroke with your mouth, or use your lips and tongue to stimulate the frenulum as you pump away. If you moan with pleasure while his cock is in your mouth, he feels the delightful vibration of the sound in his penis. Long before "Hummer" was the name of a gas-guzzling jeep, it was known as a stimulating type of blowjob. Test his music knowledge and his ability to focus by playing "Name That Tune" while you hum your way into his heart. (This may give new meaning to the term "having a tune stuck in your head.")

Try some moves.

Draw your lips into a tight circle, so there is almost a popping sound when the head moves in and out. Be extremely careful not to accidentally use your teeth once the action builds, as it can easily cause injury. You may carefully experiment with nibbling on the shaft, as some men find that erotic, but any use of teeth should be approached with very gradual and deliberate experimentation. Try sucking on his penis, creating

a vacuum-like tightness and pressure. Don't be afraid to suck hard, as many men enjoy that strong sensation. Suck on the head, or take the whole cock in your mouth and maintain the suction the entire time you slide it in and out of your mouth. Or take the opposite approach and take the penis loosely deep into your mouth, then move your head side-to-side in a figure eight so his penis is moving around inside your mouth. You can try long, hard strokes along the entire shaft with just your tongue or with your mouth, or quick light strokes with your mouth just on the head. There are an almost infinite number of ways to pleasure a cock. Be open-minded and playful, and you may continually find new ways to please your lover even after many years together. (And believe me, if you become great at giving him head he'll still be coming back for more after many years.)

Good vibrations.

Add vibrators to the mix for more variety of stimulation. Vibrators with interchangeable heads like the *Eroscillator* or *Synergy Pleasure System* can be used on virtually any of his erogenous zones, while your mouth and hands work elsewhere. Hold a *Pocket Rocket* against his frenulum as you suck on the head of his cock and tug on his scrotum. You can turn your mouth into a hot, wet penis-vibrator by holding (or by having him hold) a vibrator under your jaw. Or consider the *Tongue Joy*, which is literally a strap-on for your tongue. If your tongue is pierced, you MUST try this amazing micro-vibe with its stainless steel barbell accessory. The possibilities are limited only by your imagination.

Give me a hand.

Never let your hands lie still and go unused while you give a blowjob! I cannot stress this point enough. Use them to stroke his shaft below where your mouth is, or you can hold his cock firmly at the base while you suck, even using your hand to firmly draw his cock into your mouth further. Your hands are also indispensable when it comes to testicular and anal stimulation.

Have a ball.

Don't neglect his balls – another point I cannot stress enough! Testicular stimulation is highly erotic for most men. Try using your hands to pleasure his balls, or stroke his cock with your hand and use your mouth and tongue to lick and suck his balls. Most men enjoy having their testicles cupped or played with. Experiment with gently scratching his balls with your fingernails. It is natural for a man's balls to rise when he is aroused, and most men enjoy it when you gather their balls in your hand and pull them firmly down, drawing them away from the base of the cock. (Be careful never to press on the balls themselves.) You can use your fingers to form a circle around the base of the scrotum to hold the balls down in the sac. Also try tugging hard on the bottom of the scrotum, pulling it down away from his cock. Proceed slowly and carefully, trying gentle pressure before increasing it if he seems to enjoy it. As in all sensitive erogenous zones, there may be a fine line between pleasure and pain, and each man has his own threshold that may shift over time, so be attentive to his responses.

Knock at his back door.

A great many men enjoy anal stimulation. While your mouth is busy with his cock, gently touch the sensitive anus with the tip of your finger. If he does not discourage you, insert a lubed finger in his anus. If he responds positively, push your finger further into his rectum until you feel the prostate, which is the size and shape of a chestnut. Massage it with your finger. Use your other hand to press against his perineum, the area between the base of the penis and his anus. Between your two hands, one inside and one outside, you will be able to stimulate his prostate quite well. Many men are driven absolutely wild by this approach. If he enjoys rectal stimulation, you could take his cock in your mouth while facing him, then wrap your arms around his hips and use both hands to stimulate his rectum and anus. Hug him towards you each time you take his cock deep into your mouth and finger his anus at the same time. For many men, this is sheer bliss. Try stroking his cock with a *male masturbator* as you lick and suck his balls and finger his ass. If you really want to drive him crazy, have him insert an *Aneros prostate stimulator* or a *vibrating butt plug* while you suck his cock, then use your hands to stimulate his balls, nipples, and other areas. Talk about multi-tasking!

Give me a break!

If you've been at it a while and your mouth is getting sore, give your mouth a brief rest. Pull back and admire this gorgeous raging hard-on you created. Let your hot breath fall on his slick shaft. Stroke it lightly with your hands. Rub it against your cheek, kiss it lightly, hug it to your chest. If you have long hair let it fall over his penis. Stimulate him with vibes and other toys as you rest your mouth and hands. Enjoy this brief interlude before the action resumes.

The crescendo

By now probably you both have worked up a head of serious sexual steam. You have two choices: You can continue to build the tempo and action until he cums. Or, you can bring him down a bit, and then begin to build again. Although your lover may object at first to his runaway freight train of sexual energy being slowed down, in the end he will thank you for prolonging his delight.

If you feel he is approaching climax (i.e., he's writhing on the bed, clutching the sheets, moaning like crazy, proposing marriage -- a sure sign you're doing it right), then you might want to slow the action until he backs away from the imminent orgasm. Then slowly begin to build again. Many great dance and musical performances make use of this strategy, slowly building to near crescendo then backing off and starting slowly and quietly again. Try making use of it in your great performance in bed. Near-orgasm is a wonderful place to be! Try to keep him in that state for as long as possible, without frustrating him.

Some men cannot tolerate slowing down once they are near orgasm. However, often a more patient, experienced lover will adore this sort of dance. The process of building to near-orgasm, then having the action slow, with you whispering "not yet" into his ear in a husky voice as you slowly build the tempo again, may drive him wild. Be especially aware of your partner's responses during this process. Sometimes a man is past the point-of-no-return, and you must help him come if he seems unable to slow down. Also, even the most patient of lovers will eventually want to enjoy the grand finale. So try to pick up on signs that he is ready to cum.

The moment of truth

Assume the position. Any position that allows you to reach his cock with your mouth is game. But when you're ready for the finale, if you're not already in the ultimate position of sexual worship, kneel between his legs. When you sense he is ready to cum, quicken the pace. You should be pumping fast and furiously with your mouth or your hand if you can't move fast enough with your mouth. Timing is everything; at this point, **DO NOT** slow your pace no matter how sore or tired your mouth or hands become. Keep the rhythm going and don't stop. Make sure you pace yourself during the blowjob so that you can finish with a sprint. Virtually all men enjoy rapid-fire pumping at the end, but some men like it light and others like a firmer hand. Experiment with pressure and speed.

Don't forget his balls! Many men find testicular stimulation critical as they near orgasm. Some even enjoy having their scrotum tugged hard as they approach climax. Others are driven over the edge by anal, rectal, and/or prostate stimulation. You've spent a lot of time learning what he likes, now is the time to give it ALL to him at once!

As he nears orgasm, you will notice changes. His breathing may become quick and shallow, the sounds he has been making may change abruptly, he may arch his back and tense his muscles; he may throw his head back and clutch at you or the sheets. His balls rise so much they become difficult to move with your hand, his shaft will be rock hard, and the head of his cock will become so huge and engorged it feels as if it will burst. Do not stop pumping, and do not slow down! Keep pumping as long as he will let you. For many men the orgasm will be more intense and prolonged if you continue to stimulate them throughout the climax. At some point following orgasm, his cock may become so acutely sensitive that he will only enjoy the gentlest touch, if any. Pay attention to this sudden change.

Swallowing

Most men enjoy it when you swallow their cum. Men who have strong feelings for their lovers in particular may report feelings of intimacy and acceptance when their lovers swallow. One man deeply in love admitted to feeling a "soul injection" when his partner swallows. Although many partners are happy to oblige, some people find it difficult to do. Remember that it is a very small volume of liquid, about a teaspoon or so. The taste of semen is fairly mild, but can vary tremendously from man to man, and even for the same man at different times. If you have difficulty swallowing, you may try holding your breath and swallowing quickly. Some people find deep throating at the moment of ejaculation helpful, as he shoots his load so deep in your mouth that it bypasses the taste buds. If you absolutely cannot bring yourself to swallow under any circumstances, you can try to discreetly spit the semen into a tissue or towel. Or better yet, pull his cock out of your mouth at the last moment and have him ejaculate on your face or body, then make a little erotic show out of spreading his cum onto your body with your hands. Of course, if you are using a condom and you keep it on while he comes, you don't have to worry about any of this!

To Spit or To Swallow?

- It's your decision: Some like to take come into their mouth, some like to watch it shoot.
  Both can be very sexy.
- If you choose to take it in your mouth, you can swallow or keep a cloth or napkin nearby to spit into.
- Know your partner and make good choices. Swallowing during oral sex on an HIV-infected man has been known transmit the virus.

Afterward, some men enjoy it if you "milk" their cock by squeezing at the base and then sliding your hand up the shaft toward the head, getting out every last drop of cum and lapping it up. Other men are so sensitive after coming that they cannot stand to be touched. Most enjoy at least having their balls cupped by your hand.

What if he doesn't come?

Not every blowjob will result in ejaculation, and that's not necessarily a bad thing. Sometimes a blowjob will be part of many sexual activities you enjoy together in a given session. Not all men find it easy to ejaculate, although they may enjoy oral stimulation tremendously. If a man ejaculated recently, he may be unable to come again for a while. As a man ages, ejaculation typically becomes a less frequent occurrence and produces a lower volume of semen, although an older man may have at least as much sexual activity and enjoyment as a younger man. Fatigue, depression, distraction, and certain medications may interfere with a man's ability to come. Remember, the idea is to enjoy yourselves; there doesn't have to be a goal or end-point.

Do your homework. If you are serious about learning to give a great blowjob, there are plenty of resources out there. Many books deal exclusively with how to give blowjobs. Prefer to see the action live? Try a how-to video, or rent porn that focuses exclusively on men receiving blowjobs. Not everything may appeal to you and your partner, but you are likely to discover something new to enhance your experience.

It seems obvious, but remember to talk to your partner and ask him what he has enjoyed about your encounters, or what he might like to try. Encourage him to talk to you and guide you while you are giving him a blowjob. Ask him to let you watch him masturbate – you will likely learn something from watching how he gets himself off and you both may enjoy the performance.

However, don't be afraid to try things that are new to both of you. You may discover something that your partner has never experienced that drives him wild. Try giving a blowjob blindfolded and with your hands tied behind your back, so that you have to focus completely on using your mouth in the most creative way possible. Or blindfold him and tie him spread-eagle then torture him with pleasure, keeping him just at the brink of orgasm. Dress as a nurse and give him a sponge bath and rectal exam, or play a naughty schoolgirl and have your "teacher" spank you and make you get on your knees and pleasure him. Experiment with different positions, or scenarios where you role-play, complete with costumes. Vary your approach. And of course practice, practice, practice. Your eagerness to please is likely to appeal to him.

A note to the recipients of all this blowjob attention: If you want your lover to give you lots of head (and what man doesn't!), then make the area as appealing as possible. Make sure you are freshly bathed, and seriously consider shaving your shaft and balls. You are likely to feel sensitized if these areas are clean-shaven, and your lover will appreciate not having to contend with stray hairs as he or she pleasures you. Finally, your lover is likely to be generous in bed if you, too, are generous in bed. So don't forget to reciprocate!

10 Advanced Tips

- Take a deep breath before you take his penis into your mouth to relax your throat muscles.
- This is to prevent gagging if you think his penis is going to touch the back of your throat.
- Use your hand around the base of his penis to control how deep he goes into your mouth.
- Try swallowing when his penis reaches the back of your throat. It kind of tickles.
- You can start a blowjob when your partner's penis is flaccid and stimulate him to erection.
- Pubic hairs in your mouth are normal. Just stop for a minute to take them out & then keep going.
- Use a finger in your partner's anus to massage his prostate.
- Pop an ice cube in your mouth or a mint for extra stimulation.
- Run your hands over his inner thighs as your mouth moves on his shaft.
- Keep your teeth away from his penis, or very, very lightly rub them against him while sucking.
- Not all men come during oral sex. Don't worry if he doesn't - his orgasm is his responsibility, not yours.

Private Workshop Theme

These exciting workshops are taught at the private location of your choice with special attention to your group's wishes.

How to have a better intimate relationship:

An interactive workshop that explores the challenges of maintaining a healthy sexual relationship while offering modern solutions to this age old problem.

Head of the Class:

Get top marks on pleasing your man. This workshop will prepare you for any pop quiz that may come up.

The Linguist:

Become accomplished in languages of Cunnilingus and Pleasing your Woman. Every wanted to know just how your woman wants to be pleased...this one's for you.

Anal 101:

no explanation necessary!!!

Vibrators 101:

Learn how to pick the right one to meet all your needs.

Who am I?

A workshop that is centered around developing couples role play.

Safe Sex:

Learn how to play it safe and still have fun. (This workshop is Free to youth organizations and non-profit groups that support at risk youths)

To book your very own

Upscale Desires Experience

Contact

Nikeema Lee

Email: upscaledesire@gmail.com

THE MAKING OF A
SPIRITUAL DICK SUCKER

1

THE MAKING OF A SPIRITUAL DICK SUCKER

Why become a spiritual dick sucker? Being a dick sucker is fun. It's known to be empowering. Most men desire it as a part of sex play.

So why not?

Oh I see…it goes against your religion.

It's nasty. Only hoes and prostitutes do it. It's demoralizing to women to be subjected to. Oh I see it goes against your religion. That's why you're becoming a spiritual dick sucker and this book will help you.

Spiritual Dick Sucker-a master of fellatio who has mastered themselves. A believer in the Church of you, you are someone who knows two things to be true.

1. GOD loves me (or whatever higher universal self you believe in)
2. I am not alone (You are not separated from that universal/ GODLY force)

SPIRITUAL VS. RELIGION

Religion is a dogmatic system that teaches separation of you from GOD. Spirituality is the intimate relationship between the self and GOD. I AM HE AND HE IS ME John 14:11
A spiritual person knows, believes and applies two things for sure

1. GOD loves me
2. I'm not alone

g   u   e   s   s   w   h   a   t   .   .   .

You can suck a dick at any given time, free and clear of guilt and shame and religion. With the right training not even a Saturday Morning Call knock at the door can pull you off the head of your lover.

2

SUCKING DICK OR FELLATIO IS AN ART

I should know I've been in practice of my skills for over 30 years. Starting at the ripe old age of 7 years old! That's right 7. YES I said 7. OMG!! Yes 7. Pick your face up and let this shock you. I would add that I made him cum on my first try. I'm what you call a natural talent. Some would say born to do this; a child prodigy.

I have sucked big dicks, small dicks, black dicks, white dicks, domestic dicks, international dicks, fresh dicks, smelly dicks, dicks with big balls, dicks with small balls; I've had hairy dicks, bald dicks, fat dicks, skinny dicks. Guy's name dick and those who were just dicks with dicks heads. So much dick you would think I was a porn star. You would be wrong and nothing further from the truth.

I was an innocent kid that was taken advantage of, praised openly for my sins, left to survive on ghetto streets and found victory on my knees. You get it...on my knees. Both literally and spiritually HAHA

After years of sucking for survival, I took back my faux powers and started sucking for fun, for joy, for free. Oh gosh why me. Then when my business mind kicked in I started sucking for money! Shout hallelujah for the glory that was revealed in me.
Romans 8:18

It started off as an exchange for food and shelter. It quickly exculpated to cab fare and shoe money hustle. Once I knew I could capitalize (in a very capitalistic society) my services commanded high dollar, expensive fancy get-a-ways and diamond platinum wedding rings.

I could suck a dick in a single swallow. I could make it erect with just one lick. My Queendome Cum, my will be done.

To any dick I rocked, mic skills so good I can give chills to any witness just from remembering me. I was a dick sucking superhero. No call me the dick whisper.

If you notice in all my ego stroking I began by stating that this was a sense of power was far from real. A fake false, faux sense of self! An inflated ego, who's bubble burst when the dick I loved didn't love me back.

Picture 9 ½ inches of string black cock, thick with ancestral girth. A pretty and shiny new toy attached to a man that stood 5'10". He was lean, masculine in all the right places and sexy as hell. He was soft and strong, kind and rugged. You know the kind of man that would eat your pussy for 10 minutes strong then fuck the life out of you. Just to turn you over and give you your life more abundantly- Hallelujah.

However, there was one catch. He belonged to someone else. Yes he was married. No he was not one of those who hide his marital status. In fact he was very up front. He said;
Yes, I'm married
Yes, I love my wife
Yes, my wife is having sex outside our marriage and
Yes, I like you.
Wait. What!

3

IT SURPRISED ME TOO

I thought, "they must be swingers or some sort of open marriage." He's response was even more shocking;

No, we're not swingers [*Swinging, also known as wife swapping or partner swapping, is a non-monogamous behavior in which both singles and partners in a committed relationship engage in sexual activities with others as a recreational or social activity - wikipedia*]

No, we don't have an open marriage [please see previous definition]

No, I'm not fine with my wife cheating and

No, I'm not happy.

He continuous, "I'm here, sitting on your coach, in your home because when I'm around you, you make me feel wanted. You make me feel special. You make me feel a sense of happiness that I lost years ago. My wife has for some reason given up on TRYING. She doesn't want to try any more. I don't want to fight any more. With you, I find peace in the mist of my storm. Simply being in your presence calms my soul. Whether I'm conversing with you or fucking your face, I am relaxed. My real life is hell and you are my heaven. I'm asking you to be my refuge. Can you be my peace that passes all understanding?"

He was asking me to be his GOD. He was asking me to be his whore. He was seeking a source of life and strength. He was knocking on the door to my broken heart [read Get Intimate to understand my story] looking for a place to rest.

In that moment I learned;
1. Men have feelings
2. We all just want to be loved
3. You can find GOD anywhere

4

HE ASKED

He asked, sought and knocked and I opened, gave and surrendered. I open my legs, my throat and my soul. It was given on to him. I became a spiritual mistress, healing his damaged soul. Giving him Sunday morning joy! Sex filled with mass choir orgasms and pulpit, turn to your neighbor, Southern Baptist, speaking in tongues Pentecostal dick sucking.

Night after night, he lay prostrate upon my alter confessing his sins with his tongue. He received my word from un-high, shouting my name as I blessed him with my oral dictation speaking prophecy over his penis. We danced in the spirit. He... I... we created a bond. All be it temporary.

You see night after night we praised together and night after night he rose from my thrushing floor and took his rejuvenated soul HOME. Leaving me to question his love, night after night. Sort of what you could imagine GOD must feel when Sunday morning many cast their cares and he gladly receives them to cleanse you of your sins and renew in you a righteous spirit only to have a lip service of faith and 6 days of doubting. The next week your back at the alter begging for the same move of love you received last week.

He wasn't wrong but I blamed him for my lost emotions. I discovered that my fake, false faux power and disillusion of self as GOD wasn't actually connected to...guess what GOD. Kinda like how the U.S. dollar isn't connected to anything of real value.

I say all that to say, I wasn't happy. I was living a lie. I wasn't happy with him fucking me and not loving me. I wasn't happy with being a side chick. I wasn't happy with being hidden. I wasn't happy with the late night phone calls. I wasn't happy with empty kisses. I WASN'T HAPPY!! He was happy. He was satisfied. He was pleased. I wasn't.

I found that being a great dick sucker didn't make me happy. Being good at oral sex didn't make me greater.

In that moment I learned;

1. Heavy is the head that wears the crown
2. You can't be someone's GOD if you don't have GOD within you and
3. Nothing is more important than your own happiness.

DON'T WORRY, BE HAPPY

5

BECOMING SPIRITUAL

My next move to becoming a spiritual dick sucker was to become spiritual. I was already a dick sucker. Now it was time to make sense of myself. Now was the time to have real power, real joy, real love.

First step to spirituality knows that you're not alone. What I mean is understand that there is no separation from you and GOD. You and he are one and he lives in you (John 14:20). Let me prove it

[ROCKSTAR]

The word above, is a great word. I want you to say the word. I want you to stay the word without speaking. Say the word without making a sound.

Ok…

Did you say it?

Better yet did you hear it?

When you said the word to yourself, you hear yourself say it. You hear a voice. YOU said nothing. YOU made no sound however YOU heard it

SO WHAT DID YOU ACTUALLY HEAR? YOU HEARD YOUR GOD VOICE. YOU HEARD YOUR VOICEFROM WITHIN. IT'S A VOICE THAT ONLY YOU CAN HEAR IT'S YOUR TRUE GOD.

Some refer to it as that "still small voice." There nothing small about you. There's nothing small about the GOD in you.

Becoming spiritual is about connecting, listening, honoring and appreciating yourself. YOUR INNER SELF!

How do I connect, listen, honor and appreciate my inner self, My GOD self?

6

CONNECT, LISTEN, HONOR AND APPRECIATE

Connect

Daily, take no less than 5 minutes to just be quite. The outside world is fast and busy. It's loud and intrusive. You must slowdown the mind in order to become familiar with the sound os your inner GOD self. Every day upon waking, take 5 deep breathes in through the nose and out through the mouth. This forms a inner connection to your inner self.

Listen

Sitting or lying for 10 to 30 minutes simply listening to your voice, is the way to start. In a relax state your inner self (voice) will begin to speak. It not asking you for your opinion, it's not asking you for your feedback. It just wants you to listen. It just wants to express itself to you. It wants to reveal itself to you. Your inner voice wants to help you solve problems and give solutions to issues you may be facing. It looks to give you confidence. It wants to give you reassurance. It wants to give you praise. It wants to give you hope. It wants to give you peace. All you have to do is sit still and what... LISTEN!

Honor & Appreciate

Just like your outer self your inner self craves to be recognized. How you honor and appreciate your inner you by being Thankful and Grateful. When the inner you speaks it simply wants to be recognized, that's all. By being Thankful and Grateful for what you have been given, you show a love for yourself. Thankfulness and Gratefulness are the divine keys to happiness. When employed, Thankfulness and Gratefulness create an intimate relationship between yourself and YOURSELF. You become one with your inner GOD.

YOU BECOME ONE WITH YOURSELF

YOU BEGIN TO LOVE YOURSELF AND YOURSELF

BEGINS TO LOVE YOU

CREATING A TANGIBLE INTIMATE CONNECTION

THAT ONLY YOU CAN KNOW ABOUT

THIS RELATIONSHIP IS PRIVATE

IT'S ONE-ON-ONE

IT'S YOU AND YOU

IT'S SPIRITUAL

7

DON'T SKIP THAT PART

You cannot become a spiritual dick sucker if you're not spiritually connected. Being spiritually connected is simply being connected to yourself, your inner self and your GOD self. When you do this you will experience one thing
LOVE

This love is magical. This love is powerful. This love is the peace that passes all understanding. This is the love that will never leave you or forsake you. This is GOD's LOVE. Remember, the two things that a spiritual person knows for sure;

1. GOD loves me and
2. I'm not alone

Until you internally experience this life force, SEX will be a mere physical activity to get off and let off. Period! It is empty and devoid of real value. Kinda like that U.S. Dollar bill. Fucking becomes this childish routine played only to stroke the ego. No one is filled with anything meant to sustain a mental, emotional or spiritual connection.

Sexual partner are merely ponds and chess pieces moved around hoping, wishing and fornicating tirelessly chasing the illusion of love.

When you know GOD's love
When you know that GOD's love comes from within
When you know you're not separated from love and
In fact you and GOD are one in the same
You can be allowed to experience sexual pleasure from WITHIN

Being sexually pleased from your inner self is different. It's actually no words in the human language that can explain what it's like. We have to seem to dumb it down to one finite word common among me...ORGASM.

However it's deeper than "The Orgasm". It's greater than the orgasm. When you become spiritually connected to your inner self you can and will experience this love sexually. Becoming spiritual and having a spiritual sexual experience you will understand this next statement.

IT DON'T FUCKING MATTER HOW YOU SUCK A DICK AS LONG AS YOUR HAPPY

The tips, tools and techniques to the art of fellatio in this book are pointless, if you are living a lie by living an unhappy life. No amount of coaching will bring your soul peace and joy if the soul is not first happy.

HOW CAN I ACHIEVE HAPPINESS?

Once you're happy with yourself. You will be happy with the world around you. No matter what challenge may come your way.

The words I used are not by accident. They are designed. When you're happy it's because you're connected and bonded with the you WITHIN.

Sucking a dick is about expression. It's about expression of emotions you feel first within. The creativity needed to successfully enhance the oral sexual experience comes from the heart, a healed and self-loved heart. It comes form that still small voice from within you.

So let's recap

1. Men have feelings
2. We all just want to be loved
3. You can find GOD anywhere
4. Heavy is the head that wears the crown
5. You can't be someone else's GOD if you don't have a connection to the GOD within yourself
6. Nothing is more important than your own happiness
7. Becoming spiritual is about connecting, listening, honoring and appreciating your inner self.

You can be a spiritual being and have a sexual experience.
You can love GOD and Suck a Dick
Well...very...very...well
With passion and enthusiasm
And with LOVE!

HAPPYOLOGY

HAPPYOLOGY

Is this really a Science?

http://www.findingauthentichappiness.com/is-happyology-a-science.html

Let's see first what science is:

Science....	(from the Latin scientia, meaning "knowledge") refers to any systematic knowledge-base or prescriptive practice that is capable of resulting in a prediction or predictable type of outcome.
Logos......	"study of" - used as a suffix (logy) in most names of braches of science.

More strictly, science is a continuing effort to discover and increase human knowledge and understanding through disciplined research. Using **(a) controlled methods**, scientists **(b) collect observable evidence** of natural phenomena, record **(c) measurable data** relating to the observations, and analyze this information to construct theoretical **(d) explanations of how things work**.

As knowledge of our universe and existence grows, new branches of science are developed to deal with those areas of nature and, all of them, study how "**energy**" - the primal and only substance of everything that exists - manifests, behaves and expresses itself in a particular field, like:

Physics...	the study of energy and how it behaves as force, matter, motion (movement of energy), etc.
Biology...	examines the structure, function, growth, origin, evolution, distribution and classification of energy as living things.
Astronomy...	the study of energy expressed as celestial objects, such as stars, planets, comets, galaxies, etc.

| Neurology... | deals how energy works through the nervous system. |

I call this scientific approach **Happyology**. The study of the *essential nature* of happiness.

The term is not new, but it mainly has been used advocating people to be *happy, happy, happy* (*don't worry be happy!*) all the time, and that has been considered an unnatural condition of humans.

Happyology, as presented here is the study of the essential energetic nature of happiness expressed as emotion and feeling in living organisms.

Can Happyology as presented here, be considered a science? Let's see:

a) Can it collect **observable evidence** of natural phenomena? Oh Yes. Anyone can observe the many visible effects of happiness.

b) Can it use **controlled methods?** Yes. We can easily control methods to make us sad o happy.

c) Can it construct theoretical **explanations of how emotion work?** Of course, after all we are talking about energy and, science in general knows a lot about energy. Like any other science, Happyology relates, uses and applies tools, technologies and knowledge from several other scientific fields

d) Can it record **measurable data?** Well, the "happy-meter" has not been developed yet. We use empirical observation and easily notice emotion being strongly manifested when compared to a very mild and weak one. Personally, I don't really care much about finding out how many "units of happiness" I have towards my wife compared with "units of happiness" toward my kids or a friend! - Besides, as far as I know, there no "sex-o-meter" either and Sexology is worldwide recognized as the scientific study of the behavior and function of sexual "energy."

Having fulfilled all pre-requisites to be considered a science by itself, I officially declare, in this year of 2009, the establishment of this new science.

Welcome to the new Happyology!

This Science of Happiness is the study of energy expressed as the emotion and feeling of Happiness and all that derives from the nature of this energy and force.

NOTE: **Positive psychology**, sometimes referred also as the science of happiness, considers the importance to feel angry, frustrated and sad when it is appropriate. What Dr. Tal Ben-Shar calls, "**The permission to be human**." That is, feeling all the emotions that human being can feel as opposed to trying to tell ourselves to be happy all the time and allowing yourself to feel all emotions as they come up without getting stuck.

Some comments about this point of view are deemed necessary:

First: The idea of advocating people to be happy, happy, happy all the time gives the wrong impression happiness would be like being stuck in a unique emotional state without variation.

This is not so, for as we have explain in our section about emotion, happiness represents an extremely wide range - *infinite really* - of levels of frequencies attainable to human beings which gives an immense variety and fluctuation of emotions throughout all of them and, all of them are pleasurable.

Second: The concept that not feeling sad or angry anymore makes you no longer human is like saying it would be impossible to be always in excellent health because being human you must experience all sicknesses known to mankind. Or, like saying that I have to steal, because that is also something that other humans do and experience, therefore I have to experience it too.

Third: They say to allow yourself to feel all emotions as they come up. Come up? Come up from where? This assumes emotions come from a place over which we have absolutely no control and therefore we can do nothing about it. - That is not true. We have control over our emotions.

Our Happyology science, *based on energy handling*, recognizes the true nature and origin of what we call emotions. They all are inside us and we have a natural ability to handle our energies as we please and feel whatever we want, whenever we want.

www.ingramcontent.com/pod-product-compliance
Lightning Source LLC
Chambersburg PA
CBHW062024040426
42447CB00010B/2119